To bray or not to bray?

by Alan Davison

Shield Publishers
ISBN-13: 978-0966144123
ISBN-10: 0966144120

I suppose I should do or say something. A lot of people have subscribed to my blog. I don't want to let them down. But what should I do or say? Maybe I should do something that requires coordination and strength. Like a triple back-flip. That would be impressive! Too bad I don't have coordination and strength. Maybe I should do something funny. Like attempt a triple back-flip without coordination and strength. That might be funny. But it might hurt. I don't like things that hurt. I never have. Before I do anything I ask, "Will this hurt?" It's a good question. Another good question is, "Where's the food?" That may be the best question, because it usually leads to pleasure, unless there isn't any food. Then it's a sad question, perhaps the saddest question of all. Hmmm... I guess I should do or say something. I don't want to let people down.

Do you think my ears are too big? said Blurtso.

Too big for what? said Alex. You know, said
Blurtso, too big, too big for the ideal shape of
a donkey. I'm not sure, said Alex, what's the ideal
shape of a donkey? You know, said Blurtso, the
shape you always see in the magazines, on the
billboards, and in the beer commercials. Beer
commercials? said Alex. Are those donkeys ideal
donkeys? They must be, said Blurtso, or the
advertisers wouldn't use them. How do you know
the advertisers aren't using grotesque donkeys to
get our attention? Grotesque donkeys? said
Blurtso, I never thought of that... but if those
shapes aren't ideal, then what is? I don't know,
said Alex, maybe your shape is ideal. My shape?
Sure, said Alex, why not? Well, said Blurtso, it *is* a
fine shape, and it *has* served me well... I guess it
must be very sad... to be a grotesque, small-eared
donkey, paraded around for the world to see.

Isn't that an odd shape, thought Blurtso, staring at his reflection in the water. That nose, so round and ponderous, like a boxing glove, and that smug little smile, and those attentive, pin-point eyes. What a strange thing it is, that shape, my shape, staring at my shape, that shape. Boxing-glove nose, greyish white, grey body, dark-grey hooves, perked-up ears above attentive eyes. Tuft of hair atop his head. Atop my head. My head housing pin-point eyes looking at his head. Housing looking housing looking. Blurtso one and Blurtso two. Blurtso one and Blurtso too. Double Blurtso smiling smugly, me to me. What does he see when he looks into me? What does he think when he thinks of me? Does he think who on earth could he be? And what's the heart of this mystery?

Whew! This sun is hot! I wonder if it's dangerous? I wonder if it will make me collapse? I wonder if it will make me collapse on my side or collapse in a heap? I wonder if my nose will make puffs of dust in the sand? I wonder if I will know I have collapsed and am making puffs of dust in the sand? Whew! said Blurtso, this sun is hot!

4

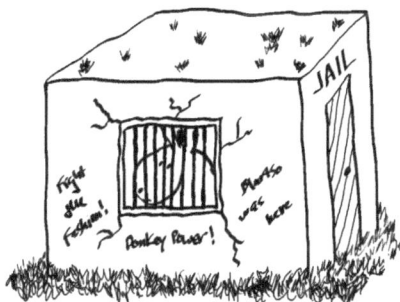

And they gathered before him and said, "Blurtso, speak to us of justice." And Blurtso replied, "There is no justice but that people must live with themselves. A good person lives with a good person, and an ass lives with an ass."

I wonder if I will like being famous? thought Blurtso. When the world is filled with Blurtso t-shirts and coffee mugs, Blurtso paintings and sculptures and smiling Blurtsos cast in bronze, Blurtso billboards and displays, neon and virtual and Christmas and Easter Blurtsos, and spin-off Blurtsos ad nauseum… I wonder if I will remember these days with nostalgia, when a simple donkey could have a simple meal, and take a nap in the comfort of perfect anonymity.

I think I will be lazy today, thought Blurtso, as he rose from a night of sound and restful sleep. Yes, that's it. Today is a good day to be lazy. The sun was shining and the morning was cool and the grass was covered with dew. But how does one go about it, how does one go about being lazy? Let me see, he thought, what does a lazy person do? Most lazy people don't move around a lot, so maybe if I don't move around a lot I will be lazy. Blurtso stood in the grass with the dew on his hooves and didn't move around a lot, and then he didn't move around a lot some more, but after a while he felt he wasn't being lazy, he just felt he wasn't moving around a lot. Lazy people also seem to breathe slowly, he thought, so he began to breathe slowly, then he breathed slowly some more. Hmm, thought Blurtso, that still doesn't feel like what I think being lazy is supposed to feel like. Lazy people also don't do jobs that they're supposed to do, so maybe I could invent a job I am supposed to do and then not do it. So Blurtso invented a job

and then he didn't do it, but he still didn't feel lazy.
In fact, after several more attempts Blurtso began
to feel that this morning was turning into one of
the busiest mornings of his life. What could the
solution be, he thought. There must be some trick
right in front of my nose. Blurtso thought and
thought and thought, and then he thought and
thought some more, but he couldn't find the
answer. I give up, he said with a snort, I don't care
if I ever learn to be lazy, and then he lay down in
the grass and drifted off to sleep.

I wonder if I should get up? I'm very comfortable
here, though it might be more comfortable somewhere else. I suppose I'm missing some exciting
things. But it's hard to miss things if you don't
know what they are. And if I did know what they
were, and was doing them, I'd miss lying in this
grass. I guess the only way to enjoy something...
is not to think about what you're missing.

There are a lot of intelligent people at Harvard.
I wonder what it would be like to be intelligent?
I wonder if it makes pumpkin pie
taste even better?

Here I go! said Blurtso, looking down at what lay below him. Here I go! he said again, still looking at all the things that lay below. Blurtso's boney little hooves clung tightly to the rocky spine on which he stood, and his pin-point eyes were bright and full of frenzy. Here I go! he said a little more quietly, and with much less conviction. Here I go! Here I go! Here I go! he repeated, and clung even more tightly to the spine that began to cut into his hooves and make them bleed. Here I go! he said more loudly, but with no conviction at all. Here… I… and off he went, slipping, sliding, and tumbling into the only future that awaited him.

O.k., said the professor, let's try number three. Two trucks, each filled with pumpkin pies, are going to the Whipped Cream Factory. The first truck leaves fifteen minutes before the second truck and drives at a speed of forty-five miles per hour. The second truck drives at fifty-five miles per hour. There is a donkey in the back of each truck. The donkey in the first truck can eat seventeen pumpkin pies in an hour, and the donkey in the second truck can eat twenty-one pies in an hour…

There are three bridges, the first at five miles, the second at ten, and the third at fifteen. Both trucks can travel only twenty miles per hour on the bridges. Each bridge is a quarter mile long. O.k., the question is... at the moment when the second truck overtakes the first, which donkey will have eaten more pumpkin pie? Who would like to give this a shot?... How about you in the front row, the one with the boxing-glove nose... Me? said Blurtso. Yes, said the professor, which donkey will have eaten more pumpkin pie? Neither, said Blurtso. Neither? They will have both eaten the same, said Blurtso. The same? Yes, said Blurtso, each donkey will have eaten as much pumpkin pie as he could.

Heraclitus, said the professor, was a Greek who

wrote, "You can't step into the same river twice..." Why would anyone step into a river? thought Blurtso, that's what bridges are for. You can't step into the same river, continued the professor, because the river is always changing, and when you step in a second time, it's a different river, and you are changing too, and are not the same as when you first stepped in. In fact, repetition is a myth, it's impossible... I'm sorry, said Blurtso, I'm afraid I wasn't listening, could you repeat that?

Remarkable! said the band master.
What an unusual interpretation of Chopin!

Let's see, said Blurtso, what's next on my schedule?
Mondays and Wednesdays, 12:00-1:45,
with Dr. Old MacDonald. My favorite class!
"Welcome," said the professor, "to Animal
Husbandry 101."

You can identify Impressionist painting,
said the professor, by visible brush strokes,
emphasis on light, and attention to movement
as a critical element of equine experience.

Blurtso de Milo

Today, said the professor, you will be given a block of clay to create a figure of your own...

The "Blurtso"

Michelangelo's "David," said the professor, is a perfect example of High Renaissance sculpture. Notice the powerful jaw-line, the proud nudity, the defiant glance...

What did you think of today's lecture, said Alex, about the seeds of revolution being inherent in the Capitalistic system? I'm not sure, said Blurtso, I must have missed that part. I was looking at a whippoorwill outside the window.

Je suis un âne
Tu es un âne
il, elle, on est un âne
nous sommes des ânes

Mon Dieu! thought Blurtso. Il y a beaucoup d'ânes dans la France!

And down the road he went, clippety clopping, stamping, stomping, tramping, tromping, and kicking up dust as he went. Hi ho, sighed Blurtso, putting one hoof in front of the other and thinking of nothing at all. Mile after mile, day after day, year after year, kicking up dust and thinking of nothing at all. What's that? thought Blurtso, noticing a cloud of dust in the distance. It looks like a cloud of dust, he said, kicking up his own dust behind him. Little by little, slowly but surely, hoof after hoof, the two clouds grew nearer. And nearer and nearer, and nearer and nearer, until the two clouds could move no nearer. Hmm, thought Blurtso, peering into the dust that was beginning to settle. What shape is that shape, peering at this shape, peering at me? Boxing glove nose, attentive eyes, dusty little hooves, with a tuft of hair between perked up ears. Hello, said a voice from the dust, I'm Pablo. "Pablo," echoed Blurtso, I'm Blurtso. Your hooves are grey and mine are brown, said Pablo. Your body is brown, and mine is grey, said Blurtso. Hmmm, said Pablo. Hmmm, said Blurtso. The road is quite dusty, said Pablo and Blurtso in

unison. Would you like to join me? said Blurtso.
I'd love to, said Pablo. And as they started down
the road, the dust that was two clouds became one,
larger than a single cloud alone.

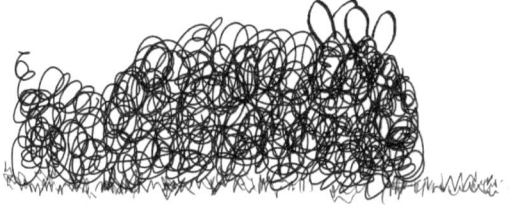

Curse these clumsy hoofs! said Blurtso.

How am I going to let the whole world know every
insignificant thought that comes into my mind?
You mean "hooves," said Pablo. "Hooves?" said
Blurtso. Yes, said Pablo. Hmm, said Blurtso, you
may be right. Let me give it a try… "Curse these
clumsy hooves!" I don't know, said Blurtso, I think
"hoofs" sounds more clumsy than "hooves." You
mean "clumsier," said Pablo. "Clumsier?" said
Blurtso. Yes, said Pablo. I don't know, said Blurtso,
I think "more clumsy" sounds more clumsy than
"clumsier."

Mmmm, said Blurtso, taking the first bite of the pumpkin pie he was eating and thinking of all the pumpkin pies he had ever eaten. Mmmm, said Blurtso, taking the second bite of the pumpkin pie he was eating and thinking of all the pumpkin pies he had wanted to eat. Mmmm, said Blurtso, taking the third bite of the pumpkin pie he was eating and thinking of the all the pumpkin pies he was going to eat. Mmmm, said Blurtso, taking the last bite of the pumpkin pie he was eating and wondering where his pumpkin pie had gone while he was eating.

O.k., said the boss, "Pablo the Gardener," what experience do you have? Experience? said Pablo. Yes, said the boss. I'm a gardener, said Pablo. O.k., said the boss, but what can you do? I can make things grow, said Pablo. Very well, said the boss, but can you do anything important? Important? said Pablo. What is more important than making things grow?

My neck hurts, said Blurtso, trying to turn his head and feeling a pain spear his shoulder. Maybe if I do some exercise it will feel much better, maybe if I do what I did when I was young.

And off he went, to do what he did when he was young. Oh no! said Blurtso. Now I can't move my back! he said, after he had done what he did when he was young.

I wonder if I'm going the right direction? thought Blurtso, walking across the field. I wonder if I'm making progress? If the world is round, the direction forward is also the direction back. And vice versa. Hmmm, I wonder who invented the idea of progress?

Off I go, said Blurtso, thinking he was going some place. And off he went, traipsing across the field on his way to where he was going, coming from where he had been. This will really be something, thought Blurtso, when I get to where I'm going. It will surely be worth the effort it will take to get there. There will be so many things where I'm going that aren't like the things from where I'm coming. And on he went, hoof after hoof after hoof, and hoof after hoof after hoof. The sun was shining, then the sun was setting, then the moon was rising, then the moon was setting, and on he went. I've got to keep going until I get there, he thought, when his stumpy little legs grew weary. And on he went, hoof after hoof after hoof, and hoof after hoof after hoof. Whew, thought Blurtso, I must be coming closer if I keep on going farther. And on he went, farther and farther, and closer and closer, and farther and farther, and closer and closer. When he could go no farther, he stopped and looked back at the trail of where he had been, and forward at the trail of where he was going. Blurtso, he said to himself, you silly ass, you'll never get to where you're going, nor back to where you've been, for you're always at the beginning of where you're going, and at the end of where you've been.

My Shakespeare paper is due tomorrow, I'd better get started. I wonder what I should write? I guess it would be too obvious to say that Shakespeare knew a lot, even though he did. He knew more than I know, that's for sure. I wonder how he learned all the things he knew? I wonder if he went to school? I wonder if he wrote papers? I wonder who students wrote papers about before Shakespeare became Shakespeare? If Shakespeare would have known how famous he was going to become, he could have written a paper about himself. That would be easy. Even I could write a paper about myself. But I don't think I'm ever going to be famous. I don't think Harvard is ever going to offer a class called "Introduction to Blurtso 101," or "Advanced Blurtso 320," or "Blurtsearean literature and the end of Enlighten-ment." At least I hope not, because I don't want to be famous. If I were famous, I wouldn't have a moment to myself. People would be bothering me everywhere I went, even in the library, and I'd never be able to get started on my Shakespeare paper, or my Blurtso paper, and I'd really better get started, because it's due tomorrow.

To eat, or not to eat,
—that is the question—
whether 'tis sounder for the stomach
to suffer the pricks and pangs
of outrageous hunger and resist,
—and by resisting, shrink this swollen shape—
or to indulge, and then sleep,
for after that indulgence, the sleep that's
sure to follow spawns decrease of increase,
and makes of energy lethargy's fool;
to eat, and sleep, and fatten as we dream!
Ay, there's the rub; for in that fatness of form
what dangers may lie—the
hypertensive extinction, the diabetic
demise—must give us pause to consider
the view of a sugary grave;
yet what burro would not exchange
a future pleasure aloof,
for a present pleasure ahoof?
'Tis a consumption devoutly to be wished,
when one of his stomach might its quietus make
with a baked pumpkin!
Thus do cravings make cowards of us all,
sugaring over the dieting hue of resolution
with sweet-scented cinnamon
and graham-cracker crust, and with this,
best intentions turn awry, losing,
in the act of consuming, the name of action.

Alas, poor Yorick, an excellent pie did he make.

Why should a dog, a rat, a human have life,
and thou no breath at all?

The future, thought Blurtso, doing his best to understand the idea. What could that be? Something that has not happened and is not happening and may not happen but will happen in a present that is not this present.

Hmm, a present that is not this present. Where does this present end and the next present begin? If I found that point, would that be the future? Blurtso did not have a very big brain, but even he knew that such a point would never be found. There is only one present, he said with confidence, even I know that.

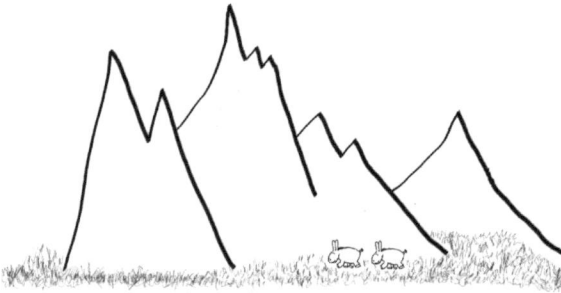

Look at that mountain, said Blurtso, mountains can be exciting! Yes, they can, said Pablo. From the top of that mountain you can see the whole valley! said Blurtso. Yes, said Pablo, but you can't see the mountain.

Happiness, thought Blurtso, sitting with his boxing-glove nose supported on his front right hoof. I see the others, he thought, moving here and there, sniffing and peering, obeying and straying, leading and following with a need on the pillow, a need that stirs them in the morning and settles them in the night. And somehow the reward emerges, from the silence and babble, from above or below, a series of notes rising, repeating in the sound of hoof after hoof after hoof.

Recycle Bin

I'd better make sure everything I use is recyclable, thought Blurtso. Let's see... I use my eyes and my ears and my nose and my hooves, and I sometimes even use my tail. Yep, said Blurtso, I'm completely recyclable.

I love the smell of wood in autumn, and the sound of dry leaves. This is a very nice log. I wonder which tree it came from? I suppose it was like any other tree, growing slowly, drinking minerals, seeking sun. I suppose birds built nests in its branches, and squirrels chased up and down. I suppose it was at the center of a universe of sights and sounds, never thinking it would fall, and be hollowed out. I guess the shell always outlasts the heart, and the forest is strewn with empty armor. And every living thing is immortal... until it dies.

Ooops, I stepped on a crack... that's bad luck. I wonder if anyone saw me? It's not bad luck if no one sees you. But I saw me. I should really try to be more oblivious.

Hello, said the devil. Hello, said Blurtso. I see you've come to buy a trombone, said the devil. Have I? said Blurtso. You must have, said the devil. I don't think I need a trombone, said Blurtso. You don't? said the devil. I already have two, said Blurtso. Two trombones! said the devil, you must be very happy! Yes, said Blurtso, I am. Do you want to give me one of your trombones? asked the devil. Absolutely not, said Blurtso. You are happier with two trombones instead of one? said the devil. Yes, said Blurtso, I'm quite fond of my trombones. Well, said the devil, if you are happier with two

instead of one, it stands to reason that you would be happier with three instead of two. Yes, said Blurtso, that stands to reason. And if three makes you happier than two, four would make you happier than three. Four trombones? said Blurtso. Absolutely, said the devil, and five and six. I'm not sure, said Blurtso, there must be a point of diminishing trombones. Diminishing trombones? said the devil. When more becomes less, said Blurtso. More becomes less? said the devil, that makes no sense. I suppose it doesn't, said Blurtso, admiring a trombone out of the corner of his eye.

Off I go, said Blurtso, following my shadow. Off
I go, following my flat friend, painting and
unpainting the prairie, darkening each step I take.
Off I go, farther and farther, stretching to a place...
where darkness... meets darkness.

A lot of people seem frustrated.
They seem to think the world, or someone,
owes them something. I don't understand that.
I feel lucky just to be here.

Being in a hurry has never
increased my enjoyment of anything.

Someone told me there was an orchard here,
that became a field of grain,
that became a forest of pitch-pines.
I wonder what donkeys become?

"Blurtso sings the donkey electric"

I sing the donkey electric!
A song of asses I sing, near and far!
Asses on hills, asses in fields, asses in herds,
more bountiful than the once-bountiful buffalo,
asses on land and asses at sea, asses short, skinny, fat and tall!
Multitudes of asses,
spanning these star-spangled states!

I have perceived that to be an ass
is to be enough.

The ears of the ass are sacred, delicate,
twitching receptacles of sound,
assiduous antennae registering, recording all,
the hooves of the ass are no less
than the slippers of sultans
striding silken alfombras and seraglio stone,
the snout of the ass and his nostrils—a dual lamp
of Aladdin—inhaling flowery fragrance,
leading to wished-for fiestas of pumpkin pleasure,
the ass's tail, though stumpy or small, and swatting flies,
is a palm fanning reclining Cleopatra,
his teeth, precious jade, are greened and polished
by the grass of a thousand fields,
his attentive eyes and friendly balance of features,
—courtly countenance and caryatid composure—
no less perfect than the visage of Helen.

Such asses I see, to the north and to the south!
From blistering bivouacs of winter
to blazing battalions of summer,
Patagonia to Peloponnese, Malibu to Manhattan,
Concord to Cambridge, every here
and every there, asses I see! Brown, grey,
yellow, red, purple, orange, azure asses!

Asses in other climes, asses in other times,
French, British, Australian, Arabian, Asian asses!

Eating every blade of grass, an ass!
Trampling every leaf that falls, a hoof!
Wading every stream that sings,
a snout, a snort, and a bray!
Hee-haw goes the jack!
Hee-haw goes the jenny!
Hee-haw go the judge and jury and judged!
Hee-haw from the dell! Hee-haw from the glen!
Hee-haw at mid-day! Hee-haw at the moon!

I see the resigned ass, bearing a load,
obeying the coax of his lord,
I see the boisterous ass braying,
in the barn, his bonny bray,
I see the amorous ass (of these there are many),
expressing exigencies by day and by night,
I see farms, fields, freeways and burgs,
each in their way, replete with asininities,
I see the asinine politician, professor, and poet,
each one leaving a brand on the asses of asses.
And the asses of yore, you ask, where are they
with their clip and clop on the stones of the street?
Les ânes voici! I say! Les ânes voici!
Heeding the whinny and neigh,
and ass-bray of the future!

What song do I sing? (you ask and I reply),
I sing the song of asses!
Certain, and stoic, and strong!
From each face an ass!
From each office, family, and farm!
Asses I sing! Avalanches of asses!
I sing! I sing a song of asses!
I sing the donkey electric!

Yes, that's how it is, thought Blurtso, walking a
mile in his hooves. That's how it is and I know
that's how it is, he said walking, the only way he
could walk, in his hooves. I might pretend to know
your hooves and you mine, one hoof after another,
after all, until we fall, you in yours and me in mine.

Uruguay is the biggest country in the world! No it
isn't said Pablo. It isn't? said Blurtso. No, said
Pablo. Then why are the donkeys in Uruguay so
happy? I'm not sure they are, said Pablo. Really?
said Blurtso. Really, said Pablo. Then I'd better go
as soon as possible! Why? said Pablo. To cheer
them up!

30

Hmm, said Blurtso, licking his hoof and turning the page of the morning paper. Let's see who did what when and why... love hate, give take, future past, slow fast, here there, then now, what when, who how, win lose, live die, settle choose, where why, fortune fame, pardon blame, smoke choke, weep joke, his hers, yours mine, rain shine, sad fine... rolls are fresh and the coffee's free, la dee da dee da dee dee.

What's this? said Blurtso, pawing up a marble. Wow... an aggie! and here's another... an opal, and a cat's eye, and an oxblood, a turtle, a ruby, and a steely! Let's play keepsies! he said, scattering the ducks in a circle he drew on the ground. If I could just knuckle down, he thought, pressing his hoof into the sand. O.k., here goes... bull's eye! he said when his taw knocked a duck off the pond. Now I'll go for that granddaddy... bingo! Now I'll get that peawee... bang! Blurtso continued to shoot, striking one duck after another until the circle was clear. Hmmm, he said, feeling as empty as the empty circle, maybe I shouldn't have won all the marbles.

O.k., said Blurtso, on three. One, two, three… Go!
And off they went as fast as they could.
Hmm, thought Blurtso, Pavlov was right.

****

Goodness me! thought Blurtso. Look at all
these runners and bikes! Maybe I should do a
marathon, or triathlon, or decathlon….
If I trained night and day,
I'm sure I could beat myself at something.

These look delicious! said Blurtso to the cook who had just made a batch of scones. Mmm, said Blurtso, biting into the steaming pillow that was dripping with honey. The cook frowned, and continued to frown as Blurtso enjoyed the scone. I think I'll have another, said Blurtso, biting into a second steaming pillow and letting the honey trickle down his throat. The cook scowled with a glance of hatred and fury. That calls for another, said Blurtso, taking and eating a third, and a fourth, and a fifth. And on it went, Blurtso eating and the cook scowling, until Blurtso reached the last scone which he plopped into his mouth and finished in one bite. Mmmm, said Blurtso, licking the honey off his mouth and hooves. Fine! shouted the cook, picking up the empty plate and throwing it against the wall. Now, what will you give me?! What will I give you? said Blurtso, still licking the honey from his hooves... I will give you the under-standing that your reluctance to share, is more selfish than my insistence to take.

Blurtso did not always wake with joy in his heart. In fact sometimes he was downright morose. This was one of those days. What's the point, thought Blurtso, of one more morning and one more afternoon, and all those minutes in between. What's the point of all that effort? Despite his spirit the sun was rising and the dew was shining on the grass. Well... he said without enthusiasm, here I go, putting one hoof in front of another... and another... and another. The sun was soaking the grass and Blurtso could feel the dew on his ankles, and the spongy earth added a bounce to his gait. Hmmmm, thought Blurtso, enjoying the bounce and the hop and feeling the air in his lungs. His shoulders and haunches grew warm and his hooves moved easily across the field. That's better thought Blurtso, skimming his nose on the grass, that's more like it he said, slipping into a trot, that's the point, he said with a smile, that's what it is, he said, hopping and skipping across the field.

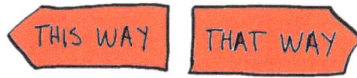

Which way is downhill?

Like my brothers, I have found time
to escape time and its burden.
I have found pleasure in distraction,
and satisfaction in its pleasure.
The fugitive light leaves a temporary trace.
One sits, another dances,
still another builds walls of silver
which another with silver shall destroy.
I walk beside the waters,
an insignificant syllable dissolving in the sand.

Well, I guess it's time to cross the river.

The river was wide and the current was strong and Blurtso could not tell how deep it was. I suppose it will wash me to sea, he thought, testing the water with his hoof. I suppose I will float for a while and then sink like a stone. I suppose I will become part of the river before I reach the sea.

I will not repeat my self...
I will not repeat my self...
I will not repeat my self...
I will not repe... ys

They seem to be repeating themselves, thought Blurtso, listening to the things they were saying. They seem to be repeating themselves. I'm glad I don't do that. Because they seem to be repeating themselves.

We don't need you anymore, Blurtso,
you're free to go. Free? said Blurtso, looking for
anything that resembled a chain.

What a lovely day, thought Blurtso, skipping
across the field. Excuse me, said a voice, but you'll
have to carry a load if you want to continue. As
you wish, said Blurtso, bending to accept his load
and walking across the field. I'm sorry, said the
voice, but you'll have to carry another. And so I
shall, said Blurtso, crouching to accept his load and
trudging across the field. And another, said the
voice. If I must, said Blurtso, kneeling to accept his
load and crawling across the field. And another,
said the voice. Whew! thought Blurtso, when he
could no longer see the day or the field or himself.
I hope everything is still waiting, when I'm free of
this load that has become myself.

That's far enough, said Blurtso, drawing a line on the ground with the edge of his hoof. The sand was dry and sun-baked and he had to scrape the surface several times before the mark was visible. That's far enough, he repeated, and the others remained on their side of the line. Blurtso remained on his side as well, looking up at the others then looking down at the ground. The sun that had baked the ground was hot and began to bake Blurtso and continued to bake the ground. One by one the others walked away. Then there was only Blurtso, the sun, and the ground... Ooops, said Blurtso, as he let his hoof slip across the line he had drawn in the sand. Ooops, he said, as another hoof crossed, followed by his haunches, his rump, and his stumpy little tail. Ooops, he said, turning and sweeping the line with his boxing-glove nose, then stamping and stomping and tromping until there was no mark left at all. Very good, thought Blurtso, as he surveyed his work and considered his new-found freedom. Freedom? he thought, looking in the direction where the others had gone. Wait for me! he cried, scampering off to join them.

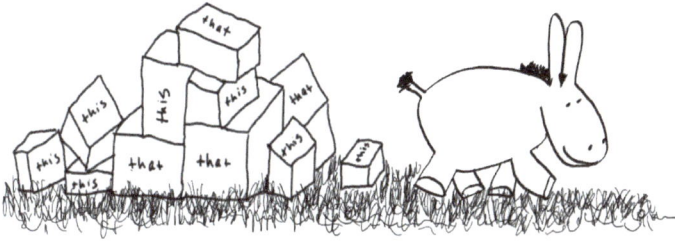

Let me see, said Blurtso, I can let go of this and that, and I can let go of that and this. Yes, that's better said Blurtso, feeling better already. And I'll let go of that and that and that, and I'll let go of this and this and this. And of course, I'll let go of letting go, he said, feeling as good as he had ever felt.

Hmmm, thought Blurtso, would you look at that, dust particles in the air, illuminated by the sun. I wonder what keeps them afloat? There must be some sort of current. Maybe it's my breath... I suppose they would settle if I weren't here. They are very pretty. I'm glad I can be of use.

Hello, said Pablo, my name is Pablo. Hello, said Bonny, my name is Bonny Bray. Bonny Bray, said Pablo. Pablo, said Bonny Bray. Bonny, said Pablo. Pablo, said Bonny Bray.

"The first time…" sang Bonny, "ever I saw your nose… I thought the sun… rose on your ears… and the moon and the stars… were the crown you placed… on the green… and the tasty fields… my love… on the green… and the tasty fields… The first time… ever I grazed with you… I felt the earth… move beneath my hoofs… like the trembling heart… deep inside of me… and I knew… you could understand… my love… I knew… you could understand… The first time… ever I napped with you… and heard your snore… harmonize with mine… I thought our song… would fill the farms… and bray… 'til the end of time… my love… and bray… 'til the end of time… The first time… ever I saw… your nose… your nose… your nose… your nose…"

Maybe we should make plans for the future, said Pablo. The future? said Bonny. Yes, said Pablo, what are we going to do? We'll be together, said Bonny. Yes, said Pablo, but what we will we do? We'll walk around, said Bonny. And then? said Pablo. Then we'll eat and drink, said Bonny. And then? said Pablo. Then we'll sleep, said Bonny. And then? said Pablo. Then we'll walk around, said Bonny. And then? said Pablo. Then we'll eat and drink, said Bonny. And then? said Pablo. Then we'll sleep, said Bonny. And the next day? said Pablo. Yes, said Bonny, and the next day. Wow, said Pablo, that sounds wonderful! Yes, said Bonny, it truly does.

The birds are nice, said Blurtso, they sound very happy. Yes, said Bonny, Pablo can identify all of them by their songs. Really, said Blurtso, what was that one? That was a chickadee, said Pablo. And that one? said Blurtso. That was another chickadee. How about that one? said Blurtso. That was the same chickadee you heard the first time, said Pablo. Wow, said Blurtso, that's amazing.

It's beautiful to love something...
that can never love you back.

The chickadees are in full throat today, said
Blurtso. No, said Pablo, those are blackbirds you
hear. Really? said Blurtso. Well… how about that
one… now *that* was a chickadee! No, said Pablo,
that was a kingfisher. Really, said Blurtso, a kingfisher? Wow… it sure sounded like a chickadee…
hold it… hold it…how about *that* one… now *that*
was a chickadee! No, said Pablo, that was a
red-tailed hawk. A red-tailed hawk? said Blurtso.
Hmm, he must have been imitating a chickadee…
hold it… hold it… how about *that* one! That was
the most unmistakable chickadee I've ever heard!
No, said Pablo, that was a duck. Remarkable, said
Blurtso. What about that, was that a kingfisher?
No, said Pablo. A blackbird? No, said Pablo. A
red-tailed hawk? No, said Pablo. A duck? No, said
Pablo. A chickadee? No, said Pablo. I give up, said
Blurtso, what was it? That, said Pablo, was my
stomach growling.

The road was dark and the trees were tall
and the wind was still. Blurtso walked
quickly, keeping to the edge of the road
where the grass muffled the clippety clop of
his hooves. The moon in the trees threw
shards of light on the ground and Blurtso
could hear himself breathe. I must try to
breathe more quietly, he thought, I must
move swiftly without haste. At the edge of
the road the branch of a tree occasionally
grazed his flank. The wind began to rise and
the jagged shadows moved on the ground.
The wind will mask the sound of my breath,
thought Blurtso, moving swiftly without
haste. The sound of the wind and the shadows of the trees are good friends, he thought,
good friends indeed...

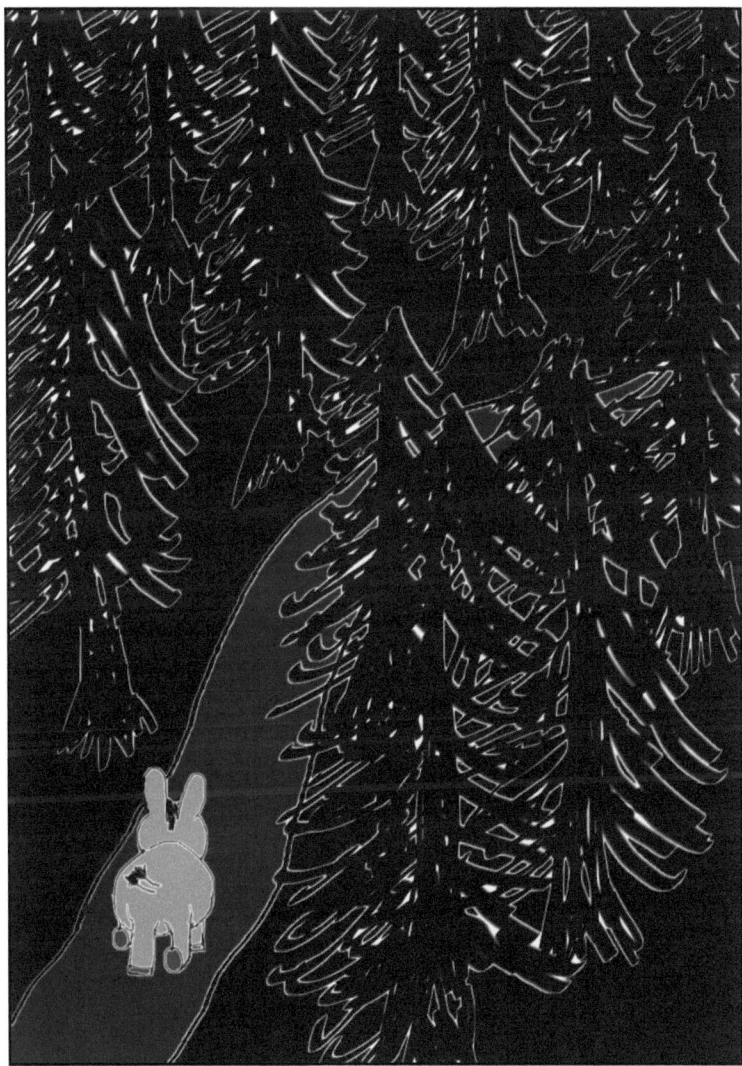

It's very dark, thought Blurtso,
and there's no one in sight.
I think I'm lost.
I wasn't paying attention and now I'm lost.
There's a light ahead.
I wish I were home.

Oh no! said Blurtso, I'm going to be fired!
How can I cover my tracks?!
I know, I'll apply for promotion!!

Thanks so much, Blurtso. I only need
your help with a couple of things…

I have only one rule when looking for a job...
beware of enterprises that require
any clothes at all.

Honk!... Honk!... Honk!...
Get off the f!@#%!g road you stupid donkey!
Hmmm, thought Blurtso. That person is sure in
a hurry. He must be out of pumpkin pie.

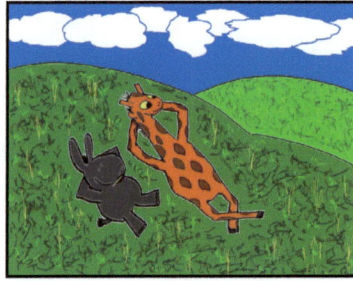

Hey, said Alex, would you look at that… What? said Blurtso. That cloud, said Alex, it looks like a human. Where? said Blurtso. There, said Alex, can't you see? That's its head, and those are its eyes, and that's its television, and its boat, its ATV trailer, and its four-car garage… Of course! said Blurtso, and what's the dark cloud next to it? That? said Alex. That's a credit card bill.

I need to become self-sustainable, said Blurtso. Let's see... at the store I can get three pumpkin pies for ten dollars... and I know a farmer who needs someone to fertilize his fields... and he'll pay me ten dollars a day to wander up and down his rows... and at the store I can buy three pumpkin pies for ten dollars...

O.K., thought Blurtso, I'd better get serious and do some living. Tell my friends and tell my family, be engaged and be engaging, be connected and accepted, broadcast every thing I'm thinking, what I am and what I'm not, what I shall and I shall not, not forgotten when I'm talking, when I'm sitting, when I'm walking, just as long as I keep talking, are you listening, are you listening??!!

Why are you doing that? said Blurtso. This? said the man on the street. I'm doing this so I can do it again tomorrow. Why do you want to do that? said Blurtso. So I can do it the day after that. And after that? said Blurtso. Yes, said the man, and after that. Oh, said Blurtso.

I lack enthusiasm
for the lack of enthusiasm.

Peace of mind
is the product of self respect.

Because I'm not separate from myself,
the only way to control myself
is to cooperate with myself.

The more I can leave behind,
the lighter my load,
and the lighter my load,
the more I can take with me.

I could do it more quickly if I improved,
and I could improve if I practiced,
but that would take longer
than doing it the way I do it now.

If you live in the here and now it makes
tasty food taste better,
pretty sounds sound prettier,
and friendly people seem friendlier,
but it also makes
mean people seem meaner.

Fairness lies in action, not in thought.

I am what I do,
and I do what the universe does.

All I've lost
I have accumulated.

Ambition is no substitute for love.

It's easy to tell if a product was made
by someone who enjoyed making it.

What's the difference between
rushing to be in fashion
and rushing to conform?

Love is not incompatible
with doing your own thing,
if "your" is a plural adjective.

As soon as I put it into words,
it ceases to be what it is.

Most points of view... are too pointed.

I imagine that imagining doing something
is different
than doing something.

If I can't voluntarily stop myself
from acting voluntarily,
I'm not acting voluntarily.

I make you think of me, therefore I am.

All that I trust... belongs to me.

Hmmm, thought Blurtso, the season is really
changing. Soon the leaves will turn yellow and fall.
And once again I'll be astonished... by the newness
of predictable things.

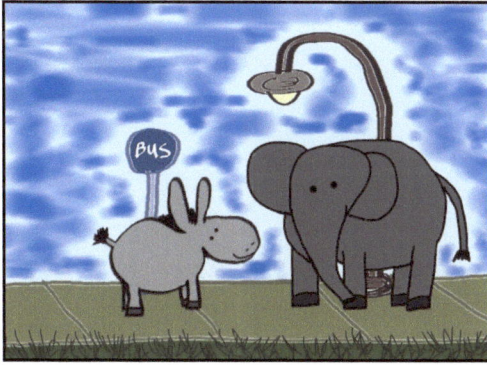

Hello, said Blurtso. Hello, said Harlan. Are you
waiting for the bus? said Blurtso. No, said Harlan,
I'm going to the river. The river? said Blurtso.
Yes, said Harlan, to watch the ducks.

The ducks are in fine form, said Blurtso.
Yes, said Harlan, very fine.

You're from Borneo? said Alex. Yes, said Harlan.
What happened to your tusks? I had to sell them to
pay for my flight. Wasn't that painful? said Alex.
Not as painful as keeping them. What do you
mean? said Blurtso. My brothers were killed for
their tusks. Oh, said Blurtso. Why did you come to
Boston? said Alex. I'm a Redsox fan, said Harlan.
Really? said Alex. Who's your favorite player? My
favorite player, said Harlan, is Big Papi. What's it
like in Borneo? said Blurtso. It's beautiful, said
Harlan, there are more plants than you could ever
eat. Do they speak English? said Blurtso. Yes, said
Harlan, in the north. Are you a Hindu? said Alex.
Yes, said Harlan. What's a Hindu? said Blurtso.
Hinduism, said Alex, is a religion that believes
elephants are sacred. Really? said Blurtso. What
religion are you? said Harlan. I don't know, said
Blurtso, what religion thinks donkeys are sacred?

I can't stop thinking about a jenny I saw at school yesterday. I saw her once, passing on the lawn, and I can't get her out of my mind. I wonder who she is? I wonder if she's a student? It's exciting to think of her, but it's tiresome, because there are so many other things to think of. But no matter what I do, all I can think of is her. And I don't even know who she is. I've seen other jennies, here and there, and now and then, but none like her. I'm dying to keep thinking of her, but wish I could stop. I've been here all day, while the hours passed, with the birds and the trees and the shadows and sounds, and I haven't seen a thing, not a single thing, because I can't stop thinking of a jenny I saw once, and may never see again. It's times like this that make me wonder... if any of us have control over anything we do.

I suppose when you see someone you like, and you don't know them, you fill in the spaces with what you hope to find. Of course, you can make reasonable assumptions. For example, she was walking when I saw her, so she must enjoy going for long walks. And she was looking around, so she must like to sit and look at things. And of course, everybody likes pumpkin pie, and whipped cream, because everything's better with whipped cream. I wonder if she likes to watch the ducks? This much is certain… she's an attentive, pumpkin-pie eating donkey, who loves long walks, probably watches the ducks, and thinks everything is better with whipped cream. She also appeared to be simple, but intelligent, and unhurried and content—I think I detected a bounce in her step—and she was clearly enjoying the grass beneath her hooves. I wonder if she likes music? I wonder if she plays an instrument? Maybe she plays the trombone. If she plays the trombone we could play duets together, and travel the world earning our passage from place to place. I wonder what her favorite music is? It's probably Für Elise. I wonder if that's her name? Elise? Or Eliza? Or Liza? Or Lizzy? Yes, Lizzy is less pretentious. Hmm, I wonder what she reads?

I wonder if she reads Shakespeare? Maybe she'll join our barnyard company. Then we could stage "Twelfth Night," and she'd be Viola and I'd be the Duke, and after many mishaps we would live happily ever after.

Hmm, I wonder what kind of donkey Lizzy likes? I wonder if she likes grey donkeys? Or brown donkeys? Brown donkeys are more colorful, but color isn't everything. I wish I were a brown donkey. I wonder what else she likes? I wonder if size matters? I know I'm not tall, but I have big ears. I wonder if I'm handsome? I don't think I'm ugly. Of course, there's not much I can do, I am what I am. Maybe I should get a haircut...

Would you look at that...
I'm already on the 18th green.

I heard you went golfing, said Alex. Yes, said
Blurtso. What did you shoot? I shot a two. A two?
said Alex. Yes, said Blurtso. That's remarkable, said
Alex. Is it? said Blurtso.

Hmm, thought Blurtso, would you look at that…
a duck in the rain. I wonder what he's doing? It's
really coming down. You'd think he'd look for
shelter, if he had any sense.

What are you thinking about? said Blurtso. I'm
thinking about Henry David Thoreau, said
Harlan. What about him? said Blurtso. He said
it takes infinite leisure to appreciate a single
phenomenon. Really? said Blurtso. Yes, said
Harlan. In that case, said Blurtso, it's good we had
a big lunch.

How are things going in Cambridge? said Pablo. Fine, said Blurtso, I saw an amazing jenny three weeks ago. Really? said Pablo, What's her name? I don't know, said Blurtso, I think it's Lizzy. You think? said Pablo. Yes, said Blurtso, I've never spoken with her. Why not? said Pablo. Because I don't know what to say, said Blurtso. Why can't you say whatever comes to mind, said Pablo, and just be yourself? Because I want her to like me, said Blurtso, and she might not like me for myself. Why would you want to be with her, said Pablo, if she didn't like you for yourself? Because she's incredible, said Blurtso. That doesn't make sense, said Pablo. No, said Blurtso, I suppose it doesn't, but maybe I could convince her to like me. That would be the *worst* thing to do, said Pablo, because then you'd have to spend your life continuing to convince her, and you'd *never* be yourself. Perhaps, said Blurtso, but at least I'd be with her. Maybe not, said Pablo, she might eventually realize you're a fake. Yes, said Blurtso, you may be right. So, said Pablo, what do you think you'll do? I'm not sure, said Blurtso, I think I'll do everything I can to convince her to like me. Yes, said Pablo, that's what I thought you'd do.

Ready? said Blurtso.
Ready, said Harlan.

Cannonball!

The bus is late, thought Blurtso. Or I'm early.
I guess I'm off schedule. I didn't plan on that. I
wonder what I should do while I wait? I could
just stand here, or I could do something. I could
take out my books and review for tomorrow.
I wonder how much time I have? If I have a
long time, I'll take out my books. If I don't, I'll
do something else. Like what? I can enjoy
almost anything for a short time. But a short
time can become a long time if you don't know
how much time. I should find something I enjoy
for a short time, and for a long time. Like what?
It's not easy when you get off schedule, and you
have to stop and think.

Blurtso's theory of evolution...

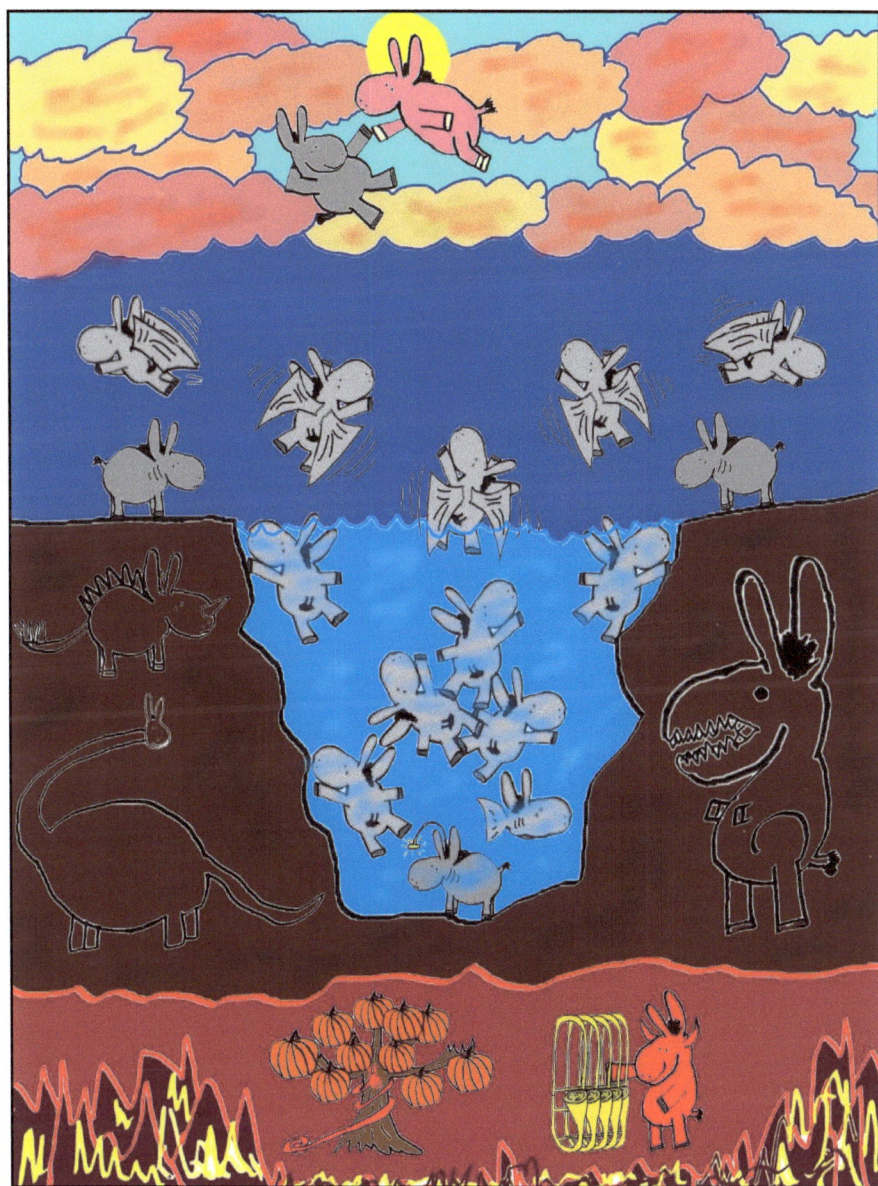

...covers all the bases.

What are those papers? said Alex. They're poems I wrote for a donkey I saw on campus, said Blurtso, would you like to hear them? I'd love to, said Alex.

"Lizzy"

A single obsession of light,
a single smile
in the soil of the soul,
a flash in the shadow,
a burning planet,
a single note from the spheres.

A single light illuminating
the water's crash
at the cliffs of the heart,
a leaping light of statues
erected and razed in the foam,
an undulating light reflecting
the swell and hollow and sway.

A simple light persisting,
in absence,
an extinguished star that continues.

"A lesson in beauty"

Because the flowers hide patiently
under the cool blanket of autumn,

because the spring comes quietly
with the sound of melting snow,

because the breeze touches softly
with the fresh fragrance of summer,

I will have to learn to see, to listen
and to feel, if I am to find you.

"The moon found you"

Caught in the discarded straw on the floor,
the broken rays reached toward you.
Like timid fingers they touched lightly,
then relaxed embracing your ankles.

Slowly, like a child entering water,
you were immersed in the light.
It moved like a gentle river
illuminating your cool flesh,
it flowed to the eddy of your knees
and grew in two rich currents
to meet at the top of your thighs.
Pausing, rising and falling with your breath,
tender waves rolled to your neck,
caressing your forelegs and breast.

As the light reached your eyes
I feared it might wake you,
so I blocked it with my hoof
and let you go on sleeping.

"In an instant"

Easily,
in an instant,
you could have not been born.

You could have had nothing.

You could have lost
the sun, the sky,
the slow moon ascending,
and the harmony
and flicker of leaves.

You could have lost
the rain's splash
exciting the soil,
the blue beyond,
and the light
and absence of light.

You could have lost everything.

And I could have lost the same,
never knowing the cure
for thirst in a world without you.

"It is early"

Of course, it is early.
You will hear other voices
sing other songs.

You will choose one.

You will come to know
the depth of the shadows
in the grasses.
You will see friends
grow and wither,
and dreams and sorrows slip away.

Will you forget these songs?

Will they vanish in the beauty
with which they cannot compete,
the white mountain, the red rose,
the resolute eyes of a lover?

Or will they remain,
and remind you of the glow
your eyes had once,
and the magic they inspired
in the heart of another?

The last flower is gone,
but somewhere its seed remains,
and when the seed is gone,
its flower will remain.
I suppose nothing is whole unto itself.
We are all just vehicles,
and life moves through us.

****

I wonder how many snowfalls I've seen… and
how many more I'll see. I suppose there are those
who watched the last one last year who won't
watch this one this year—those who won't ever
watch one again. I suppose it's up to me… to do
the watching for them.

I wonder how long it will snow? I wonder how much it is snowing in the mountains? I wonder if there is ice on the stream or if the snow is falling on the water? Snowflakes don't last very long in the water. Unless there is a rock. Then the snowflakes can land on the rock. I wonder if snowflakes look for rocks in the stream? If I were a snowflake, I would look for a rock in the stream. It would be sad if I were a snowflake on a rock, to watch all the other snowflakes land in the water. I think I would prefer to land in the water. Then I could be happy for all the snowflakes that landed on rocks.

****

The snow is collecting on the frame of the windows. Collecting, melting, and collecting. I wonder if my windows are laminated? It's quite warm in here, so they must be laminated. I wonder how much energy I've stored from my solar panel? I'm glad I have straw. Straw is a good insulator. I could be warm in the straw even if my windows are unlaminated. I should make a thermos of chocolate while I still have power. I could be happy with straw and a thermos of chocolate even if my windows are unlaminated and I don't have power. Hmmm… the snow is really collecting on the frame of the windows.

It's a new year... I guess I'd better make a
resolution. Let's see… "this year I resolve to…"
hmm… "I resolve..." hmm… what does that
mean…? To be "resolved," to be "determined,"
to be "unyielding in one's purpose," to be
"intransigent," "inveterate," "obdurate," and
"inflexible." Hmm, I don't really like that. I
think being flexible is the key to happiness.
Of course, flexibility implies rigidity, that is,
something to be "flexible" about. Hmm… what
I need is a resolution that is both rigid *and*
flexible… I know!... "This year I resolve… to be
less resolved."

I wonder if anyone else likes to watch the snow like I do? It's kind of like watching a movie. Maybe I should make some popcorn to eat while I watch...

I wonder if anyone else likes to watch popcorn pop like I do? It's kind of like watching a movie. Maybe I should make some popcorn to eat while I watch...

Isn't this Hip-Hop 101?

Glissade… pas d'âne… assemblé.

Pirouette… un, deux, trois, quatre,
cinq, six, sept, huit…

Wow, what a great idea! You think so? said Blurtso.
Absolutely! What will you call it? Well, said
Blurtso, it's a toss up between "Blurtselia" and
"Donkey Lake."

Un, deux, trois… jeté!

Hmmm...

Hmmm...

Hmmm...

What have you been doing lately? said Alex. I've been standing in the snow, said Blurtso. Standing in the snow? said Alex. Yes, said Blurtso, standing in the snow.

Welcome to tonight's discussion sponsored by "The Campus Institute of Political Seriousness for Enhanced Living in an Unenhanced World." I'm your host, Jonathan Well-born Truington III, and joining us this evening is Mr. Blurtso Lundif, a third-year diversity fellow at Harvard College, who has garnered attention in Cambridge as, "the donkey who stands in the snow." Please tell us, Mr. Lundif, if you would, what is your opinion of the current political climate in our nation's capital? The political climate? said Blurtso. Yes, said Mr. Truington. I don't know anything about it, said Blurtso. Do you think, said Mr. Truington, that the politicians should all go stand in the snow? It couldn't hurt, said Blurtso. And what have you accomplished, said Mr. Truington, by standing in the snow? Accomplished? said Blurtso. Yes, said Mr. Truington, what have you learned? I've learned to stand still, said Blurtso. To stand still? said Mr. Truington. Yes, said Blurtso. Anything else? said Mr. Truington. Isn't that enough? said Blurtso. Well, said Mr. Truington, I suppose it is... and where exactly do you stand? Anywhere, said Blurtso. Anywhere? said Mr. Truington. Yes, said

Blurtso, anywhere that's snowy and cold. Is there something, said Mr. Truington, that inspires you to do it? Yes, said Blurtso, it's compelling to stand in a public place that is empty… and where, if someone does appear, they move so quickly they may as well not be there. I see! said Mr. Truington, standing in the snow is an indictment of the modern world and its frenetic pace! Is it? said Blurtso. Does it bother you, said Mr. Truington, if others stand in the snow next to you? No, said Blurtso, as long as they don't ask questions. Questions? said Mr. Truington. Yes, said Blurtso, about why I'm standing in the snow. Of course, said Mr. Truington, and apart from your scathing attack on people in a hurry, what other statements are you trying to make? Are you attempting to draw attention to a charitable cause? Are you trying to see how long you can stand before collapsing? No, said Blurtso, I go home whenever I want. And how do you know, said Mr. Truington, that it's time to go home? As soon as I start walking, said Blurtso, I know it's time to go. Remarkable, said Mr. Truington. Well, ladies and gentlemen, there you have it, neither ice, nor sleet, nor snow will stop this remarkable coed from making his stand. Please join us next week when our featured speaker will be Somerville's own self-deprecating playwright and hairbrush salesman, Reverend Willy J. Loman.

I wonder why it seems that everyone I meet is busier than me? I go to school, keep up with my classes, give my time to charitable causes, and help friends in need… but I still have time to sit and watch the snow. Maybe donkey years are longer than human years, and a donkey's day is seven times longer than a human's.

There goes another snowflake, said Blurtso. I like to watch things that fall—leaves, feathers, snow-flakes—things just a little heavier than air. There's something relaxing in watching them let go, something soothing in their acceptance and lack of direction, their trust in the cycle... of soil and stars.

I wonder how far a snowflake can fall? I wonder
if it changes along the way? I wonder if it starts
big and gets smaller, or starts small and gets
bigger? I wonder if it thinks it has control over
where it's going, or if it thinks it's directed by
gravity and wind? Maybe gravity and wind are
within it, and it does control where it's going.
And the things that create gravity and wind are
also within it. And a snowflake determines not
only its own course, but the course of time,
matter, and space.

I feel lonely, thought Blurtso. I guess that's natural.
Donkeys are herd animals. I haven't been in a herd
for a while. Maybe I should go to the Mall, or
Harvard Square, which has become the same thing.

Hey… footsteps in the snow. I wonder where
they're going? Maybe I'll follow them. Doo dee
doo dee dee, dee dee dee dee doo… hey, what's
this? No more footsteps. I wonder what happened
to the person who was making them? How can a
person just vanish like that, and make no more
tracks? Hmmm, maybe I'd better go see Harlan,
and make sure he's alright.

Hello, said Blurtso. Hello, said the counselor, have you decided on a major? No, said Blurtso. Well, said the counselor, maybe I can help. What do you like? I like everything, said Blurtso. Everything? said the counselor. You can't major in everything. Why not? said Blurtso. Because you have to specialize. Why? said Blurtso. So you can graduate. Why do I have to graduate? So you can get a job. A job? said Blurtso. Yes, said the counselor, in your specialization. Hmm, said Blurtso. Can I avoid all that... if I major in logic?

Hey, this is easier than it looks!

Well, I saw Lizzy yesterday, and now I'm right back where I started… anxious… yearning… happy… sad… hopeful… hopeless… exhausted… inspired… a total wreck… with a twisted knot in my stomach… isn't love grand.

I wonder what I should be when I grow up? I can't be a student forever. Unless I go to grad school. But grad students look terrible. They have rings under their eyes like they've been living in a cave. I guess they're worried about their grades. And when they graduate they worry about getting a job. And when they get a job they worry about getting pro-moted. And when they get promoted they worry about retirement. All because they can't eat grass.

Still thinking of Lizzy? said Harlan. Yes, said
Blurtso. What would you do, said Harlan, if you
were actually with her? I don't know, said
Blurtso, I think I'd just snuggle up to her, brush
her shoulder with mine, and nibble her ear...

It's hard to believe, on a night like this, that
anything's alive beneath the snow and ice, that
the remnants of summer still sleep in the grass.
Hard to believe there will ever be music again in
the trees, and a lonely heart will ever be healed.

What are you doing? said Harlan. I've decided to immortalize Lizzy on canvas, said Blurtso, I call this, "Jeune âne au piano."

"Lizzy se baigne"

"Lizzy embrasse son chien"

O, she doth teach the torches to burn bright!

It must be midnight, said Pablo. I can hear the last
train to Boston. Imagine all the people, staring out
the windows, seeing their reflections in the glass...
and the darkness beyond. I wonder what they're
thinking?

****

After dark there are only sounds to mark time, and
the reflection of the waning fire, and the last ker-
nels of corn... the night animals will be out. In the
morning I'll see their tracks in the snow. It must be
exciting, moving quietly through the snow, feeling
the pulse of your heart in your temples, seeing the
hills in the grey light, and hearing the slender
sound of the creek. And next week we're going to
Mexico!

Welcome to Mexico!

Hello, said Blurtso.

The breeze rising off the bay
is quite pleasant in the evening.

Wow, what a night... I probably shouldn't have
danced on the table, or swung from the chande-
lier, but I was so happy when the Nachos arrived.

I wonder if the sand is hot? It was warm four hours ago. The breeze is nice. It feels good on my ears. It's hard to hear over the waves. I can see Pablo talking with the parasailing people, but I can't hear a word he's saying. I wonder if he's going for a ride? I wonder if I should have another pumpkin-colada? The first one was excellent. And the second and third ones were even better. I wonder if I should call for the waiter? Wow! There goes Pablo! He's really soaring! I hope he's strapped in. I wonder what it's like up there? I wonder if he can see me? I wonder if he can see the waiter? Maybe he can get the waiter's attention. He seems to be waving his hooves quite wildly. He must be signaling the waiter. What a good friend. My pumpkin-colada will be here soon.

I can hear Bonny and Pablo playing in the pool. They sure sound happy. You can't blame them, you can swim right up to the bar. I'll have to join them, as soon as I rest up from my siesta.

I got one!

From the edge of the bay I leave you the silence
of a wave after it has broken,
and before the next one breaks.

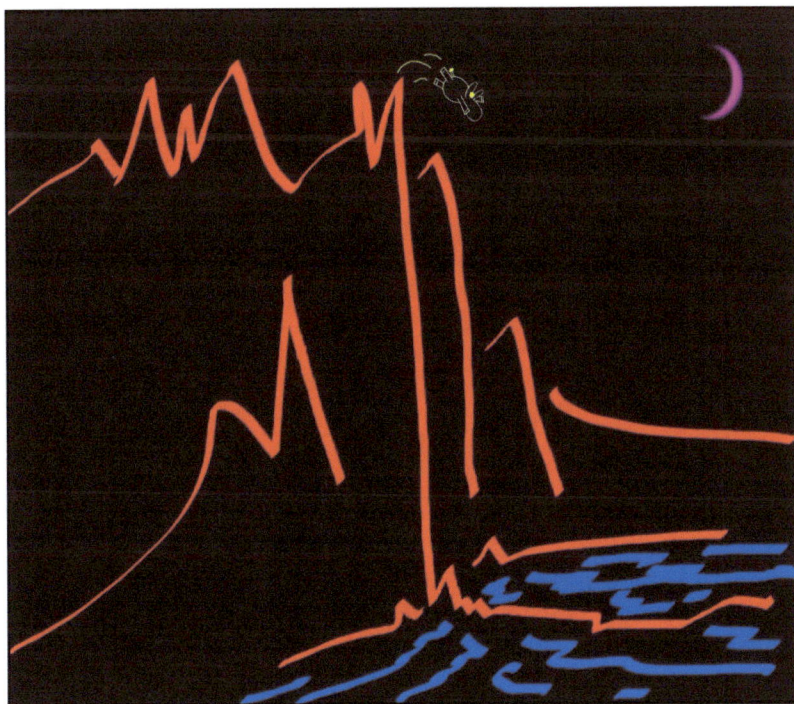

Burros arriba!

Doo dee doo dee doo, dee dee dee dee dee,
swimming with the fishies, diving in the sea…

Hey! There's my cufflink!

"Volver, volver, volver,
a mis calabazas otra vez."

Pardon me Sir... passengers are allowed only one carry-on trombone.

I'm sorry, said the attendant, no electrical devices during takeoff.

Vegetarian? said Blurtso. Yes, that's mine.

Hello, said the customs agent. Are you bringing any fruit into the country? Any vegetables, plants, seeds, or insects? How about animals or wildlife products? Cell cultures? Snails? Soil? Have you been on a farm or in close proximity of livestock? Fruit? said Blurtso. No, I don't have any fruit.

Hmm… it's starting to rain. I wonder if I should go into a shop. If I do I'll probably miss my bus, and then I'll have to wait for the next one. And if it keeps raining I'll miss that one and have to wait for the next one, and the next one… hmm... and then it'll get dark, and the shop will close, and they'll throw me out after the last bus leaves, and I'll have to spend the night in the rain, and in the dark… hmm... unless I hitch-hike, but no one will stop for a wet donkey, unless someone does, someone who has bad intentions, or owns a forced-labor copper mine... and I'll be donkey-napped and flown to the mine on a private jet smuggling military secrets, and I'll be forced to work night and day, living on coca leaves and betel nut, knowing that the future of the world lays in my hooves, if I can only escape and steal back the secrets... and I'll have to bribe the guards, and slip into the hills and build a raft... and sail it to the sea where I'll board a steamer... and I'll cross the Atlantic, until the ship hits an ice burg and sinks... and I'll climb into a lifeboat which I'll sail through the wreckage pulling out survivors... and they'll all be grateful, all but the one who is a guard from the mine and has been following me, and is going to kill me the minute we reach Greenland… hey it stopped raining!

I have spent my life eating things that are alive
or were once alive. I sure hope whatever I become
food for... enjoys eating me as much as I have
enjoyed eating.

It's unsettling to get up before dawn, when it's still
dark and the barn and the yard and the neighbor-
hood are quiet. It's like I'm the only living thing on
the planet, and it's hard to believe others are
waking to the same darkness, seeking refuge in
artificial light, bathing and dressing... getting ready
for the day they trust will arrive.

Somewhere beyond this city, maybe up north, in Maine, the warmth is thickening on the breeze, the mud is hardening underhoof, and voices are swelling on the branches. And a donkey with no place to go is losing himself, in the fragrance of damp earth and pine.

Bonny was talking a lot about mindfulness yesterday. I wonder what she meant? I wonder if it's anything like stomachfulness? I'll have to ask her the next time I see her, if I'm not too focused on the present to remember.

Sitting in the woods can be suspenseful, said Blurtso. Suspenseful? said Pablo. Yes, said Blurtso, as if something is about to happen. What do you expect to happen? said Pablo. I don't know, said Blurtso, it's as if the continual sound of the creek, the breeze on the ears, the deep alterations of light and dark, are all waiting for something… maybe a change in the wind or a change in the sky, a sudden downpour or wild animal, maybe a cougar come to drink at the stream… something dramatic is going to happen. COME AND GET IT!!! called Bonny from the cabin. FRESH SCONES AND PUMPKIN PIE!!!

Hello, said Blurtso, are you Lizzy? No, my name is Beatrice. Beatrice? said Blurtso. Yes, said Beatrice. Didn't I see you at Harvard? Probably, said Beatrice, I'm a student there. But your name's not Lizzy? No, said Beatrice, it's Beatrice. Oh, said Blurtso, but you like to go for long walks? No, said Beatrice, I prefer to run. Do you like to sit and look at things? No, said Beatrice, I almost never sit. But you must like pumpkin pies? No, said Beatrice, I've never tasted one. Are you waiting for the bus? No, said Beatrice, I'm waiting for my beau.

Well, said Blurtso, I guess that's that.

Hey, thought Blurtso, my ears cast a shadow, like
the shadow of a sundial, moving around the
lawn... It's a quarter to three. I guess the poet was
right, we *are* made of time.

Occasionally, I free my mind to the day,
I feel the sounds, the colors, the breeze,
and I remember this day, which is every day,
a lifetime.